BES
Graduation
2005

May These words be
your Confession.

Mr Whitman

Ms. Vermillion

THE CREED

WHAT YOU BELIEVE
AND WHY

-|-

MICHAEL BAUMAN

Published in Nashville, Tennessee by Thomas Nelson, Inc.

Library of Congress Cataloging-in-Publication Data
is available.

Printed in the United States of America

1 2 3 4 5 – 06 05 04 03 02

Contents

"Stand at the crossroads, and look, and ask for the ancient paths,
where the good way lies; and walk in it, and find rest for your souls."

Jeremiah 6:16

Can you define your Christianity? Do you know what you believe? What are the essentials of faith? Can you give an answer for the hope that is in you? *The Creed* offers a foundation of faith. The truths of the Bible are summed up in the Apostles' Creed, one of the oldest declarations of faith known to the church. This book will walk you through the Creed, offering simple explanations in each section. *The Creed* will bring you closer to God by showing you the story of your salvation.

As a Christian, you share your faith with people from all over the world and from all different walks of life. Each chapter in this book includes testimonies from real people of all ages. All of them share ways that the Creed has affected their lives and deepened their faith. Your life can be changed as well. Join the centuries of Christians before you who have proclaimed "I believe."

I am pleased to acknowledge here the support, assistance and encouragement I received from John Feneley, Alun Thornton Jones, and Thomas Richardson, all of the Centre for Medieval and Renaissance Studies, Oxford, where the bulk of this book was written, as well as the generosity of Hillsdale College, which provided me with the sabbatical time and money needed to bring this text to completion.

I am especially grateful for the generous assistance given me by John Reist, Thomas Burke, Duane Beauchamp, and Jon Corombos of Hillsdale College, Michael Williams of Dordt College, Donald Williams of Toccoa Falls College, John Franke of Biblical Seminary, and Maurice Kelley of Princeton University. Their sharp eyes and keen minds kept me from lapses and infelicities of various sorts.

Michael Bauman

"As the Lord's Prayer is the Prayer of prayers,
and the Ten Commandments are the Laws of law,
so the Apostles' Creed is the Creed of creeds."

Philip Schaff, *Creeds of Christendom*

What is a Creed?

A creed is a confession, a declaration, an affirmation. A creed takes that complex collection of historical narratives, poems, prophecies, sermons, letters, visions, and parables that we call the Bible, and summarizes them down into a handy statement. A creed is a summary of the fundamental teachings of Scripture and a personal statement of religious convictions. It is a way for the church to say "this is what we believe the Bible says." A well-written creed marks out the truths that the Bible reveals and requires for salvation.

Creeds find their basis in the Scriptures. Many of Paul's declarations of faith have found their way into various creeds written over the centuries. "For us there is one God, the Father, of Whom are all things...and one Lord Jesus Christ, through Whom are all things, and through Whom we live" (1 Cor. 8:6). Also, "I delivered to you first of all that which I also received: that Christ died for our sins according to the Scriptures, and that He was buried, and that He rose again the third day according to the Scriptures" (1 Cor. 15:3-4). Paul encouraged his readers to "hold the traditions which you were taught" (2 Thess. 2:15). These statements in Scripture are called "the pattern of doctrine" (Rom. 6:17) and the "model of sound words" (2 Tim. 1:13). Every creed of note affirms these truths.

The Apostles' Creed

The Apostles' Creed is the most widely used summary of Christianity the church has ever composed. It is time-tested, historically rooted, and widely accepted. Because of its simplicity, the Creed is remarkably suitable for teaching and for learning. In fact, the church has looked to the Creed for theological instruction and practical guidance for centuries.

Tradition holds that the Creed was named for the apostles because, in solemn assembly, each of the twelve contributed one of its twelve articles before they left Jerusalem on their various missionary journeys. Although this is just pious fiction, it makes a nice story. The Apostles' Creed is anonymous—there is no record of its authorship.

The Apostles' Creed has the great virtue of being simple and brief. Its restraint is admirable in comparison with some of its more rambling relatives. Its conciseness makes it more serviceable than longer confessions. Perhaps an illustration will help make the point. The first time I traveled in Switzerland, I did so on a bicycle. I knew before I ever saw the Alps that Alpine travel by bicycle would be both rewarding and demanding. I tried to pack my gear accordingly. I did not want to drag several pounds of equipment that I would never use over the towering mountain passes of Switzerland. I wanted no more than I needed. Unnecessary baggage is a burden, not a blessing. The Apostles' Creed carries no more theological baggage than is strictly necessary.

*for Doug Bowman
who knows what it means
to say "I believe"*

The Apostles' Creed

I believe in God the Father Almighty,
Maker of heaven and earth;
and in Jesus Christ His only Son our Lord,
who was conceived by the Holy Spirit,
born of the Virgin Mary,
suffered under Pontius Pilate,
was crucified, dead, and buried.
He descended into hell.
The third day He rose again from the dead.
He ascended into heaven,
and sits at the right hand of God the Father Almighty.
From there He shall come to judge the living and the dead.
I believe in the Holy Spirit;
the holy catholic church;
the communion of the saints;
the forgiveness of sins;
the resurrection of the body;
and life everlasting.

"*I Believe...*"

Credo

"My prayer time always begins with the Creed. After that, I say my own private prayers. At first, I thought the 'memorized' prayers were only stepping-stones to the 'real prayers. However, it has been increasingly evident that the opposite is true. To have my faith rooted in an eternal and unshakeable ground, I needed to join an unbroken communion of saints. 'I believe in God, the Father Almighty.'"

Pastor Scott — Phoenix, Arizona

Personal Faith

" **I** " From its first word, the Apostles' Creed is personal. It is a declaration of individual faith. Though all Christians share common beliefs, the faith we confirm in the Creed is to be our own. We speak for ourselves, and not for anyone else.

By beginning on this personal note, the Creed puts some emphasis on individual responsibility. As a child of God, we have the privilege to stand and say "I believe." We do not stand entirely alone, though. We are a part of the "communion of the saints" mentioned later in the Creed. Though we speak for ourselves, we speak in concert—in unison—with all the church.

When we stand in the congregation on Sunday mornings, raising our voices together to recite the Apostles' Creed, our own voice rings in our ears. In the midst of a crowd, this becomes an

> "*Jesus posed a question to the man who was born blind. 'Do you believe in the Son of God?' The reply was simple. 'I believe'*" **John 9:35, 38.**

intimate moment with God, a time of rededication and an affirming of our faith.

Two Sides of Faith

Faith has two parts. It is made up of both assent and trust. The difference between these two sides of faith is sometimes described as the difference between saying, "I believe that..." (which is an assertion) and "I believe in..." (which is trust). Put a little differently, faith can be called both a rational commitment and an act of confidence—both a knowing and a doing.

Assent

Assent is the intellectual portion of our faith. It deals with what we believe—the content of our faith. Believers do not abandon their senses in order to take a leap of faith. Despite what skeptics might say, Christians are not pinning their hopes on empty wishes or flights of fancy. The Christian faith is neither ignorant nor unreasonable.

We were not given minds just to ignore them. Studying God's Word takes both discipline and a bit of mental application. Someone who claims to have faith but refuses to learn about the truth of God's plans will be a target for any charlatan who comes down the pike. Christianity has its very foundations in reason and truth. Our belief is supported by the hard facts of history. Peter urges Christians to be able to give a reason for their hope (1 Pet. 3:15). Paul's way of saying this was to assert that he knew the One in whom he had trusted, and because he did, he was con-

"*I have believed in God since I can remember. Looking back, I can see His hand in my life, guiding me and protecting me. How could I do anything but love Him!*" **Muriel, age 60**

vinced that his future was secure (2 Tim. 1:12).

Trust

The second element of faith deals with our relationship with God. Faith isn't just understanding the facts. Anyone can memorize a list of beliefs. What counts is using your faith. In fact, if you do not act upon your faith, your faith should be called into question. Claiming to have faith without commitment is not sincere. It is hypocritical. Christian faith is not only knowing; it is

> "*I wasn't introduced to the Apostles' Creed until I took a basic theology course in college. We were required to memorize the Creed, and then challenged to write a new creed of our own. It was tough. I have a great appreciation for the writers of the original creeds.*" **Lynda, age 36**

doing. James says that faith that isn't backed up by action is dead (James 2:17). A living faith is even willing to suffer hardship for the sake of the truth.

So, while sound reason and commitment to fact constitute the intellectual side of faith and serve to protect the believer from being led astray, the trust or commitment side of faith is that which gives it life. Trust prevents belief from being merely a mental exercise.

Source of Faith

The Creed declares the faith of a person in a Person. Christian faith is nothing in and of itself. Faith is first of all a work of God. It depends upon God as its source. Our faith arises in response to God's revelation, in response to God's initiative, and in response to God's offer. The faith that ends in commitment to God begins with the will and grace of God. Faith is the echo that God's call creates in the hearts of those who believe.

*"God the Father Almighty,
Maker of heaven and earth."*

Deum Patrem omnipotentum; Creatorem Coeli et terrae

"I remember learning to recite the Apostles' Creed
as a child. As an adult, it has become a part of my
daily life. It is for me the 'prayer of beginning.' It is
the prayer that reminds us of the essential beliefs that
make us Christian. It is the prayer that places us
before God, not asking or even thanking. It is the
prayer in which we pledge our beliefs before man and
God. It is the foundation of belief that establishes a
place for faith to take root and grow strong"

Dan — Nashville, Tennessee

God Revealed Himself

Any man who keeps silent remains a mystery to his companions. As soon as he speaks, though, people catch a glimpse of his character, intentions, skill, and personality. The same was true of God. As long as God remained silent, He was both unknown and unknowable—but God has not remained silent. He has spoken to us through His Son. Jesus is God's eloquent and gracious statement to a fallen world. This is why the Scriptures call Him the *Logos*, or Word (John 1:1). In Jesus, God speaks directly to the deepest needs of the human heart, making known to us His righteousness and His merciful intentions. If He had not made this first step, we could never have known the Father's love.

> *"My Daddy was a strict man, but he loved us kids and we all knew it. He would line us up on Sunday afternoons and quiz us on our Sunday school lessons—all eight of us! He was the one who made sure that we all knew the Apostles' Creed—every last one of us."* **Maggie, age 55**

Twisting Truth

In our fallen world, sometimes what we call "God" is often not God at all. Instead, we are pursuing a twisted truth. Because of sin, our thoughts about God often have little resemblance to the one true God. In many ways, the god in our minds is simply a mental idol, a reflection more of ourselves than of God.

11

> *"Father is my favorite name for God. It immediately reminds me that I serve an intimate God who loves me in a very deep way."* **Jenny, age 31**

There is only one God, and He is not man-made. He cannot be adjusted to suit our plans. Far too often we fall away from the first Commandment, which prohibits having any other gods but God. We may not do it consciously or intentionally. Nevertheless it is done, even though we know—deep within us—that the gods of our own making are always unsatisfactory.

Father

The supreme name of God is "Father." Everything we understand about God begins there. Once we embrace God as our Father, suddenly all of creation becomes our family home. Then we become God's own children, redeemed by Him to live with Him forever.

We did not invent the idea of God as our Father. God did. His fatherhood is unique to the one true God. The idea that God is a father is rooted in the Hebrew Scriptures and is confirmed in the New Testament. Jesus constantly refers to God as "Father"— beginning at the age of twelve, when He told Mary and Joseph that He had to be about his Father's business (Luke 2:49). Even at the very end of His earthly life, as Jesus hung on the Cross, He commended His spirit into His Father's hands (Luke 23:34, 46). When Jesus taught His disciples to pray, He began by acknowledging God as Father (Matt. 6:9). There was virtually no other name by which Christ spoke to God or of God.

Jesus Shows Us the Father

Jesus said that to see Him was to see the Father. He and the Father were one. In this way, Jesus defined His Father for us. Jesus' entire life was an expression of obedience and suffering, culminating in victory over sin and the grave. In all this, God's heart is displayed. Jesus was living proof of the immeasurable love of the Father— and of His infinite power.

Through Jesus, the God of Israel became our "Abba," an ancient Aramaic word for "Daddy" (Gal. 5:6). The true God was not the abstract, impersonal, first cause or prime mover described

"*You, O Lord, are our Father;*
Our Redeemer from Everlasting is Your name."

Is. 63:16

> "My parents adopted me when I was a little baby. Now I am adopted by God too. He is my Father in heaven. That makes me really happy."
>
> **Alex, age 8**

by ancient philosophers. Yet He was more than the exalted God of Israel, Who thundered from the mountaintop and Whose face could not be looked upon.

Paul explains that Jesus is the "express image of the invisible God" in this universe (Col. 1:15). So even though no one has ever seen God, we know Him because His Son has made Him known (John 1:18). With Christ's example before us, we can grow to resemble our Father in Heaven and our Brother at His right hand as we live on earth (Rom. 8:29).

"God is my heavenly Father. It has always amazed me that God would choose me—accepting me into His own family circle. Knowing that my welcome is secure with Him has always given me great peace." **Agnes, age 74**

"Father" Is the Very Nature of God

God has been our Father for all of eternity past—it is part of His very essence. He brought us into existence, and we can always depend upon Him. As our Father, God is constantly working to make us—each of us—His children. He is constantly striving to make a family of us. He cannot relent until He has succeeded because it is His character.

When we become His children, we are welcomed into a rich heritage. Our membership is secured in a family much more extensive, important, and enduring than any human family could be. From Him, our being and blessings descend, and to Him, we can turn our minds and hearts in utmost love and gratitude. When we become His children, we enter into a relationship that showers us with His love, intimacy, and care.

God as "Maker of Heaven and Earth"

God is described as the Maker. At His command the universe came to be. With God as our Father, we have a home. We are privileged to have a place in His divine plans. We are not merely specks in a complex universe. No indeed. We are witnesses of the wonders He has formed, drawn to applaud the Creator and sing His praises.

"*and in Jesus Christ His only Son our Lord*"

Et in Jesum Christum, filium ejus unicum, Dominum nostrum

"The Apostles' Creed is one of the
most succinct biographies ever written
about the life and purpose of Jesus,
and one of the most complete statements of one's beliefs. It says it all.
The brevity of the Creed allows for
deep, personal meditation and con-
templation—it is a gateway for you
to take yourself someplace beyond self
and closer to God."

Peter — Clifton Park, New York

Uniqueness of the Son

When we confess "and in Jesus Christ His only Son our Lord," we naturally think of Jesus' life, which is the basis of our Christian faith. These words are the center of the Creed and the heart of our knowledge of God.

Believing in a god is not at all unique to Christians, but believing in God as He is revealed in Jesus Christ is unique. Faith in Jesus Christ is what gives our religion its distinctive shape and flavor. Faith in Him is something we do in obedience to the command of both the Father (1 John 3:23) and the Son (John 14:1).

The Name of Jesus Christ

The name Jesus is a translation of the Hebrew name Yeshua, which means "God is Savior" or "God is Deliverer." Joseph and Mary gave that

"*Whenever we say the Apostles' Creed in our church, I feel as if I am renewing my vows to Jesus.*" **Alyssa, age 24**

name to Jesus in obedience to the angel's command: "You shall call his name Jesus, for He will save His people from their sins" (Matt. 1:21). Just as His name explains, Jesus is our salvation. Through Him, we enjoy fellowship with the Father, we are redeemed from bondage to sin, and our eternity in heaven is secure.

Jesus is also called "Christ." This is a name derived from the Greek word meaning "anointed." Christ is also the Greek equivalent of the Hebrew title "Messiah," which describes Jesus as the servant of God who is set apart for the high purpose of redemption. He is the One promised long ago to the patriarchs and to the prophets.

Jesus declared that He was the Messiah, the Anointed One. Inside the synagogue of His own hometown, He recited the words of Isaiah: "The Spirit of the Lord is upon me, because He has anointed me to preach the gospel to the poor. He has sent me to heal the brokenhearted, to proclaim liberty to the captives and recovery of sight to the blind, to set at liberty those who are oppressed, to proclaim the acceptable year of the Lord." He assured His listeners that these words

"God's gift to His wandering children was priceless. He gave Himself. The Apostles' Creed says that He gave up His only Son—the enormity of such a sacrifice!" **Bob, age 45**

> "*Just hearing the name 'Jesus Christ' makes me feel humbled and awe-struck at the same time. There is power in that name!*" **Joe, age 67**

were being fulfilled in their very presence, before their very eyes (Luke 4:18–21; see also Is. 61:1).

This wanderer through ancient towns and villages, and traveler of dusty roads was a penniless, wayfaring preacher. Yet when we express our belief in "Jesus Christ," we are declaring Him both "Son" and "Messiah." We are in agreement with Peter's great confession to Jesus: "You are the Christ, the Son of the living God." As Christ told Peter, this confession of faith comes from God, and we are blessed by it (Matt. 16:16, 17).

The Beginnings of Christianity

The combination of Hebrew and Greek in the name of Jesus Christ describes His universal significance to all people. He came for both Jews and Gentiles alike.

By acknowledging Jesus as the Christ, the long-awaited Messiah, we recognize the Jewish beginnings of Christianity. We recognize that through the history of ancient Israel, God was at work, calling out a chosen people for His purposes. His own entry into human history was precisely planned. We know that we are the spiritual heirs of Israel's history, its promises and its hope. This awareness of our Jewish roots gives us a fuller appreciation of Jesus the Messiah because we understand that the Incarnation was no accident. It was the result of centuries of preparation, both inside and outside of Israel.

The coming of Messiah was something God willed from before the worlds were made. It hap-

> "*I know now that Jesus was a common enough name in New Testament times. But that does not keep it from being so very precious to me now!*"
>
> **Lois, age 49**

pened in fulfillment of God's covenant promises to His people at a time when all things were ready and the world was ripe (Gal. 4:4).

The Misunderstood Messiah

Through Jesus, God carried out His plans to redeem mankind. He is the very One who found no room in the inn at His birth, and who found no reception in the house of Israel during His years of public ministry. Yet Jesus was God's Anointed Deliverer.

> "*Jesus, my Lord, my God, my all, How can I love Thee as I ought?*" **Frederick William Faber**

At the time of His coming, many Israelites misunderstood what kind of Messiah they were waiting for. Many Jews expected a national hero, a king, and a great warrior. Others expected a supernatural messenger of the world's end. In Jesus they got someone Who was all these things and none of these things. What they got was Isaiah's suffering servant—a Messiah who conquered by dying, healed our anguishes with His own, and preached about the Kingdom of God.

Jesus frequently tried to distance Himself from the faulty views many people had about Him. As God's Anointed One, Jesus knew better than His followers just what His work entailed.

Only a small group of believers understood that He had a difficult path. None could bear to think He would face the humiliation of the Cross.

God's intention for His Anointed One was global. God's purpose always was to gather all things together in Christ. He is the One under whose authority all things shall be placed and by whom all things, even now, hold together (Heb. 1:13; Col. 1:17).

Jesus as Our Lord

Calling Jesus "our Lord" is the very essence of the Christian faith because it connects us both to Him and to His will. Even the angels proclaimed Him "Lord" on the first Christmas (Luke 2:11). Paul and his colleagues also declared it when they were dragged before the authorities (Acts 17:7). When we call Christ our Lord, we acknowledge our duty to revere Him and obey Him. We willingly shape our lives around His will because we know that He has the right to rule us—and we have the privilege to obey.

The earliest Christians were faced with a profound and far-reaching decision: choosing between *Kyrios Christos*, which means "Christ is Lord," or *Kyrios Kaisar*, which means "Caesar is Lord." Paul regularly taught that someone other than Caesar was Lord—Jesus Christ. Paul seems to have understood that when we declare Jesus as Lord, it frees us from being bound to any earthly master. It was a lesson Paul never forgot. Even in old age, when he was imprisoned for his faith, he called Christ the "King of kings and the Lord of lords" (1 Tim. 6:15).

"Lord" was used even in the Old Testament to describe the Supreme God (Gen. 15:7; Ex. 6:2). Jesus rightfully owned and accepted the title: "You call me Teacher and Lord, and you say well, for so I am" (John 13:13). Christ is Lord of the world. Every part of human life is under His

> "*Jesus was truly awesome. He did so many amazing things while He was here. So many people loved Him. I can hardly wait to meet Him face to face someday.*" **Amber, age 15**

dominion—including our minds, our hearts and our consciences. He is Lord of all. He holds sway over the whole universe. Christ is not simply my Lord, or even the Christian Lord. He is not even the greatest Lord among many lesser lords. He is the one Lord. Nowhere can one find a hiding place or a Christ-free refuge (1 Cor. 8: 6). Though the world does not yet confess that awesome fact, someday it will (Phil. 2: 9–11). Before Him every knee one day will bow.

Jesus as God's Son

As God's Son, Jesus was the perfect expression of the sort of people we ought to be and of the way we ought to relate to God. When Jesus uses the word "Son" in the New Testament, He points to His unique and intimate relation to the Father. When others call Him "God's Son" in the New Testament, they also are referring to His divine origin, His divine mission, and His divine nature.

In Jesus Christ, God gives Himself to us most fully and irreversibly. In Jesus Christ, God has left His footprints in human history. Christ is the perfect example of God. God is the God of Jesus and the God who is in Jesus.

"who was conceived by the Holy Spirit, born of the Virgin Mary"

qui conceptus est de Spiritu Sancto, natus ex Maria virgine

"Learning the Apostles' Creed was a requirement in my ninth grade confirmation class. The Apostles' Creed was the beginning step in understanding my God. And now on Sunday mornings, I am not just reciting the Creed, I am renewing my pledge to God—it is a very powerful moment for me."

Marilyn — Seattle, Washington

> "When I was little, my grandmother taught me to say three different pieces from memory—the Lord's Prayer, the Twenty-Third Psalm, and the Apostles' Creed. I have never forgotten them." **Ruth, age 51**

No Ordinary Baby

To new parents, the birth of their baby is a miracle and a cause for great celebration, but the birth of one particular baby has been celebrated more than any other. Over two thousand years ago, God broke in upon human history as a baby named Jesus. He lived, breathed and walked among us as Emmanuel or "God with us."

The best word to describe the birth of Jesus is extraordinary. God became a child, and that child

32

became a man, a man who willingly bore the sins of the world upon His shoulders. Like a cloudburst over parched fields, the Messiah arrived just in time to save us. In Galatians 4:4, we read, "When the time had fully come, God sent His Son, born of a woman." The birth of Jesus is central to all of history—our calendar even pivots around it. Christ is the pinnacle of God's revelation.

By the Holy Spirit

Jesus was born by the free act of God and by the conception of the Holy Spirit. When God sent His Son into the world for the purpose of our redemption and reconciliation, that entrance was accomplished in a special way.

The Greek and Roman gods of the time were rather famous for their supernatural offspring. The sons of the gods, like Hercules or Cupid, were made famous in the legends of the people. Unlike these myths, however, the accounts of Christ's birth come from actual people who lived. Only two people—Joseph and Mary—knew the first-hand story of Christ's birth, and those stories are preserved for us in the Gospels. The first, which is found in the Gospel of Matthew, is from the perspective of Joseph and deals humbly with the entire incident in only about eight verses. The second account, in Luke, is from the perspective of Mary. Many biblical scholars have noted that the account in Luke is far more Jewish in language and flavor than the rest of Luke's Gospel and might possibly have come from Mary herself, whom Luke easily could have known. In fact, Luke says that his accounts have their origin in eyewitness reports (Luke 1:1-2).

In Luke, we read that the angel who appeared to Mary told her, "The Holy Spirit will come upon you, and the power of the Highest will overshadow you; therefore, also, that Holy One who is to be born will be called the Son of God" (1:35). The

> "*Christmas is my very favorite time of year. I still remember when I was a young girl and I was chosen to play Mary in the annual Christmas pageant. I was so thrilled. Every girl had wanted the part. It was just like long ago, when every Jewish girl hoped to be the mother of the coming Messiah. I wonder if Mary was as thrilled?*"
>
> **JoAnn, age 63**

same Holy Spirit who was active in the creation of the world, giving it life from God, also was active in the world's salvation, "overshadowing" a young Jewish maiden and impregnating her with life from above. In the first instance, the creation took place on a cosmic scale; in the second, it took place within Mary, though this time for the purpose of redemption. In both cases, however, the same divine love was at work. God's creation always serves as a signpost pointing us toward God; it is a means of reconciliation because what comes from God leads back to Him again.

The Virgin Birth

The Virgin Birth of Christ has been a wellspring of inspiration for writers and artists for many centuries. It has been the source for some of our culture's most enduring expressions of beauty and piety. Unfortunately, our society today has made a god of sex, and some of our age's most flagrant doubts seem to center on the Virgin Birth. Within God's design, the Virgin Birth offers a close look at the Hand of God in the lives of His children—and serves as a rock of faith for many.

The church has called Mary "the Receiver of Life" and *Hodrigitia*—"the Guide"—because she was the one who raised Christ. Mary showed Jesus the way from birth to adulthood. She gave to our Lord physical life and nurtured significant portions of His intellectual and spiritual training. She whom God nurtured, nurtured God.

In Scripture, Mary is described as a humble and pious young Jewish woman. She was a grateful sinner who rejoiced in her redemption: "My spirit has rejoiced in God my Savior" (Luke 1:47). She was a modest and discreet person—a chosen woman, not a goddess. Her conduct and character set her apart, but she is not exalted between the Trinity and the human race. As the mother of Jesus, Mary was entrusted with a unique and sacred charge. The fact that Mary gave birth to the Son of God proves not only the Virgin Birth but also the genuine Incarnation and Jesus' full humanity.

> "*Mary and Joseph were so brave. Their faith was amazing.*" **Marlit, age 28**

Acts of Faith

No doubt Mary's pregnancy was unexpected, highly embarrassing, and nearly disastrous for her relationship with Joseph, her fiancé. It must have been equally troubling for Joseph. When he discovered that his betrothed was pregnant, he made up his mind to separate himself legally from her, though because of his love for Mary, it probably tortured him to do so. Despite the tearful objections and heart-wrenching explanations of innocence Mary probably gave, Joseph remained resolute in his desire to follow the Law of God. He did not relent until he was instructed to do so by an angel (Matt. 1:20). He then had compassion for Mary and married her, and later he willingly decided to uproot himself and his family in order to flee to Egypt for their safety. Both Joseph and Mary acted on faith with conviction, compassion and obedience. The story behind these few words of the Creed has poignant, even heroic, dimensions, which inspire many Christians in their faith.

Christ's Humanity

Born to Mary, Jesus was genuinely and completely human, except that He did not sin. The Scripture repeatedly points out Christ's sinlessness. But like us, He was subject to growth and perfected by suffering. Hebrews 5:8 says that He learned obedience. He grew in wisdom, stature, and knowledge. He found favor with God and man (Luke 2:40). Christ endured the life in a fallen world and overcame temptation, giving us an example to live by.

Our redemption required Jesus' Incarnation, suffering, death, and Resurrection. It certainly cost more to redeem us than to create us. When we consider God's selfless action in human history, we see that God drew near to us. In return, He asks us to draw near to Him.

Both God and Man

In Jesus Christ, we see both the human and the divine. If Jesus had been God only, people probably would have fled from the pure holiness of His presence. By the grace of God, His terrifying holiness was clothed in human flesh, making Him approachable. If He had been merely a man, He never could have spanned the gap between God and us. He never could have given us access to our heavenly Father. Jesus' birth is where our fallen and sinful race meets the God who reigns in righteousness. The Incarnation is the marriage of heaven and earth.

> "*When I was in the second grade, our Sunday school teachers decided that we should all learn the Apostles' Creed together. As incentive, they told us we could each earn a silver dollar and a sack of penny candy once we could say it. I don't know which was the better motivator, but it only took me three weeks to memorize the whole thing!*"
>
> **Douglas, age 69**

He was conceived not from below only, but also from above. When we say that Jesus Christ was "conceived by the Holy Spirit" and was "born of the Virgin Mary," we profess the dual nature of Christ's earthly existence. In other words, we acknowledge our belief in the two-sided beginning of Jesus Christ's life and work among us—His divine conception and His human birth.

"suffered under Pontius Pilate, was crucified, dead and buried. He descended into hell."

passus sub Pontio Pilat, crucifixus, mortuus et sepultus.
Descendit ad infernum

"As I prepare to be treated for cancer for the second time in less than ten years, I consider two statements of faith important in getting me through each day. They are the Apostles' Creed and the Lord's Prayer. Saying one or both of these through the years has helped me endure the challenges of the disease and treatment."

Eddie — Norfolk, Virginia

No Greater Love

The Creed leaps from the birth of Jesus to His suffering and death. It isn't that His years of ministry are unimportant. Rather, in the sacrifice of Christ we discover God's love most clearly. Jesus had already made clear that no greater love can any man show than to lay down his life for his friend (John 15:13). But in Jesus' case, His life was given for His enemies as well. This is what love looks like.

The Cross of Christ also shows us the horrid face of sin, because in order to banish it from the world, the Holy One had to die.

He Suffered

The last moments leading up to Jesus' death are summed up in two words—He suffered. Jesus endured the full measure of human agony. The specific suffering mentioned here is not the pain of crucifixion and death. This is the suffering that

> "Christ allowed these injustices to pull Him into suffering for two reasons. One, as a remedy for sin. Two, as an example for behavior, in cultivating obedience, patience, and courage." **Thomas Aquinas**

followed His capture and arrest. Jesus was beaten, mocked, whipped, spat upon, stripped naked, falsely accused, falsely judged, and crowned with thorns. He was then betrayed, abandoned, and denied by His closest friends.

The suffering of the Messiah was prophesied from the very beginning (Gen. 3:15). Isaiah foretold of the Savior's wounding for our transgressions, His oppression and affliction on our behalf, and His lamb-like journey to the slaughter (Is. 53:3-10).

Pontius Pilate

By naming Pontius Pilate, who was Roman procurator of Judea from 26-36 A.D., the Creed identifies for us both the time and the place of Christ's death. Pilate is not named in order to shame him forever, but to give the passion of Christ a historical anchor. The Christian faith is deeply embedded in human history.

The Jews were under Roman domination at the time of Christ, and the law prevented them from handing down a death sentence. The Jewish

"Jesus' death on the Cross is the best gift anyone could ever give me. He chose to die for me on earth so that I could be with Him in heaven forever." **Amy, age 16**

"'What is truth?' Pilate asked, and it serves him right that he should be put there in the middle of the Creed, as if the church were determined to go on saying to him, to the end of time, 'Here, you fool, this is it!'" **Ronald Knox,** *The Creed in Slow Motion*

leaders who wanted Jesus dead were forced to bring their prisoner before Pilate to get the verdict they wanted. Jesus was dragged before the Roman procurator on trumped up charges of blasphemy and sedition. Pilate found no fault in Him and told the Jews so (John 18:38). Yet, Pilate did not release Him. Succumbing instead to political pressures and the clamor of Jesus' enemies, Pilate eventually gave both the order to scourge Him (John 19:1) and to have Him crucified (John 19:16). For that, Pontius Pilate's name lives in infamy.

Crucifixion

Innocent though He was, Jesus was sentenced to execution. Pilate allowed Him to be sent to the Cross. In the days of Jesus, crucifixion was a distinctly Roman form of torture—an exceedingly cruel one. Death was certain, but it came with an excruciating, almost idle, slowness. Christ endured unspeakable pain for several agonizing hours. People who were walking by probably looked up at the Cross and thought they were seeing a thief getting what he deserved. Little did they know that He was our greatest benefactor, getting what we deserved.

More awful even than the pain that wracked His body was the suffering in Jesus' soul. The Father turned His back on His Son, and left Him to die alone and forsaken. That moment of abandonment was the deepest abyss of Christ's suffering, when He cried out "My God, my God, why have You forsaken Me?" (Matt. 27:46) The high priest had already offered the answer to His question earlier. He said that it was expedient that one man should die for the people, so that the people would not perish (John 18:14).

Death

Jesus was executed. He drew His last breath in agony. His heart stopped beating, and He gave up His spirit with a loud cry. Jesus died.

The punishment for sin is as old as the world itself. It was the verdict brought down on Adam and Eve for their disobedience—if you sin, you die (Gen. 2:17). Paul repeated this in the New Testament. "The wages of sin is death" (Rom. 6:23). In other words, it costs something to sin. The price is high indeed. Jesus' death demonstrates that it also costs something to forgive.

> *"It is rather shocking to realize that God became so vulnerable that His life was in danger. To save us, He came so close to us that we were able to kill Him. God actually died."*
>
> **Michael, age 44**

He Chose to Die

In all this, Jesus did not simply get killed. No man took His life from Him. He laid it down of His own accord (John 10:18). Willingness did not necessarily come easy for the Son of God. He prayed for His Father to take the bitter cup away. After great anguish of heart, and in the face of crushing fear, He chose death. He could have backed out at any moment. Taunts for Jesus to call down the angels could have been silenced with the appearance of the heavenly host (Matt. 26:53). But He stayed on the Cross. He could have escaped, but He chose not to.

Payment for Sin

Atonement. After the Fall and sin, we were hopelessly separated from God. Jesus was our second chance. Christ's atoning death extends as far as the curse of Adam is found. It covers every sin completely, fully, and finally. His brutal death was something He tasted for every man (Heb. 2:9). His death was a ransom paid on behalf of us all (1 Tim. 2:6). "God was in Christ reconciling the world to Himself" (2 Cor. 5:19).

What happened to Jesus ought to have happened to us. He endured divine wrath. He caught the deadly bullet upon which our names were written. He took our place. The Lord did not escape death. He endured it. He conquered it. He transformed it. He made it a door to life. By

> "*That long Saturday after the Crucifixion must have been a dark day for Jesus' disciples. They were accustomed to hearing Jesus teach them on the Sabbath, but that day must have seemed so very quiet.*" **Sandy, age 57**

dying, He paid the price for sin, and mercy for sinners is now possible. It is available to anyone who will repent and believe.

Buried

Near the end of the day, two men rushed to Pilate, begging permission to take Jesus' body. Joseph of Arimathea, along with Nicodemus, wished to give their beloved teacher a proper burial. After the day's humiliation and horror, it was the least they could do. Joseph offered his own tomb, and Nicodemus supplied a hundred pounds of fragrant spices. Anointing and binding Jesus' body with linen strips was the final farewell of disciples who were heartsick and confused. The rock was rolled into place and the mourners turned away towards their homes as the sun began to set.

Descended into Hell

Jesus died, was buried, and then descended into hell. He who became sin for us endured the just punishment for sin. He experienced hell. We have Christ's own word on the condemnation of hell (Matt. 23:33). He warned that many would be cast into the unquenchable fires there (Mark 9:43). Jesus tasted the very wrath that He warned of: "I will show you whom you should fear: fear Him who after He has killed, has power to cast into hell; yes, I say to you, fear Him!" (Luke 12:5).

As the bearer of all sin, Jesus was condemned to the consequences of that sin—hell. However, Peter declares in his first sermon on the day of Pentecost, that God did not leave His Son to languish in Hades (Acts 2:31).

"The third day He rose again from the dead."

Tertia die resurrexit a mortuis

"Our church began the tradition of reading the Apostles' Creed aloud together each month as a part of the Communion service. I was a young mother then. As my children and I became more familiar with the wording, bits of the Creed were committed to memory. Eventually, even my youngest could lisp through the phrases with a little prompting. As each grew and placed their faith in Christ, they knew exactly who they were trusting and why. What a joy to hear my family tell the basics of their faith with confidence."

Lucy — Noblesville, Indiana

The Third Day

Christianity in a nutshell—Christ has died; Christ has risen. By stating that Jesus rose "on the third day," the Creed fixes the Resurrection for us in time. This was not a mystical event, veiled in shadows and vague reports. The Resurrection was a matter of historical fact, more well-attested than any other, even in the ancient world. Jesus' Resurrection on the third day was predicted in the Old Testament Scriptures. Jesus even made His own prophetic announcements on the subject (Mark 8:31; John 2:19-21; 10:18). He was as good as His Word.

Numbering the Days

To our way of thinking, three days equals seventy-two hours. This leads to some confusion on the timing of the Resurrection. The Jews had their

> "*Of all the holidays, Easter is my favorite time of year. During a season when everything seems fresh and new, people are everywhere hearing about how they can find newness of life. Resurrection Sunday brings fresh hope.*" **Glenn, age 35**

own way of numbering days. Any part of a day is counted as that day. Jesus was crucified and buried on a Friday. He remained in His tomb for the rest of that first day and all of the second day. Then, on Sunday morning, the third day, He was raised.

This third day, a Sunday, was adopted by the apostles as their holy day. In celebration of the Resurrection, the first day of the week became known as the Lord's Day (Acts 20:1; 1 Cor. 16:1-2;

> "*Up from the grave He arose; with a mighty triumph o'er His foes; He arose a victor from the dark domain, and He lives forever, with His saints to reign. He arose! He arose! Hallelujah, Christ arose!*" **Robert Lowry**

Rev. 1:10). This set the Christians apart from the Jews, who continued to worship on Saturday, the day of Sabbath rest.

A Turning Point

Until this point, the Creed has focused on Jesus' descent, beginning in the heavens. From that exalted place He came down to earth, to be born in humble surroundings. As a man, He was put to death as a common criminal, finally plummeting into the depths of hell itself. Yet in two words—"He rose"—everything changes. Indeed, nothing is ever the same again

Jesus comes back to life, back to earth, back to His friends and family. He returns to the world that He came to save. Forgiveness, justification, and resurrection are guaranteed for those who believe in Him (Rom. 4:25; 1 Cor. 15:17-18). This is the gospel. This is the Good News.

This portion of the Creed is the heart of the Christian message. If Jesus had not risen, then everything the Creed asserts after His descent into hell would have to be ignored. Without the Resurrection, Christianity would be no more. That is what sets it apart from any other religions. Our living Savior is unique. The path to the grave led back to life again for Jesus. With faith in Jesus, our path will lead to life as well.

The Resurrection

That first Easter Sunday, three women made their way to the tomb, only to find the stone rolled away and the body of Jesus missing. An angel was on hand to ease their minds. Jesus was alive! The apostles, a little skeptical, performed their own inspection. Though linens remained behind, the grave was indeed empty. Doubt was soon set aside, though, for Jesus appeared to the startled group (Luke 24:37). This was not a ghost, no phantom, no vision, nor wishful thinking. Overwhelmed by the evidence, His disciples had to admit that Jesus was risen.

The Days Following

Jesus was seen in all sorts of places and circumstances after the Resurrection. He met His disciples while they were gathered together. He met some on an individual basis. Jesus came to them during the day and at night. He came to

> "On Easter Sunday morning, when our congregation gathers early for a sunrise celebration service, we have a tradition. Our pastor greets the assembly by calling out 'He is risen!' As a group, we all reply 'He is risen indeed!' I love that tradition." **Bethany, age 17**

them while fishing, while walking, and while eating. From downtown Jerusalem to the Galilean countryside, He was met by both men and women. People spoke with Him, touched Him, ate with Him, drank with Him, listened to Him, and kept appointments with Him. He was undoubtedly alive.

As the Book of Acts unfolds, we are

> *"I know that the Apostles' Creed has been around for a long time. It feels kind of neat to know that I am making the same pledge that Christians have made for centuries."* **Marge, age 43**

introduced to a very changed group of men. The disciples are no longer confused and dejected. Their trembling is replaced by death-defying courage. A holy boldness grew out of their own experience of the power of God. If God could raise Jesus, He could do anything. So unshakeable was their faith, that all of the disciples, except for John, went on to die brutally—martyred for preaching the gospel.

The power that transformed the disciples has never diminished. It can make us people of courage, of conviction, of purity, of power, and of victory.

Overwhelming Evidence

The Gospels record at least nine appearances of the resurrected Christ to His disciples. Paul himself mentions six in his letter to the Corinthians (1 Cor. 15:5-9). One of those was to a group of more than 500 people at once. Those who were not His followers also saw Jesus. The Roman soldiers stationed at the sealed tomb gave testimony about the Resurrection (Matt. 28:4, 11-15), and they had no reason to invent stories. They had to be paid off to tell people otherwise.

All the Jews or the Romans needed to do to squelch the rumors of the Resurrection at the outset was to produce the body. When it could not be discovered, the Jewish leaders resorted to bribing the guards on duty to say that the

> "*In the Resurrection of Christ, eternal life and eternal death were locked in mortal combat—life won.*" **Matt, age 19**

disciples had stolen the body away while they were asleep. The obvious fact that sleeping men are not convincing witnesses to events that allegedly happened while their eyes were shut doesn't seem to have occurred to them.

The Resurrection of Jesus is too extravagant a thing to invent and too well-attested to deny. It really happened.

Its Significance

Just as Jesus' body was raised and His body was altered, our perishable and dying bodies shall one day be transformed. Our mortality shall put on immortality. In the briefest of moments, in the twinkling of an eye, we shall all be changed (1 Cor. 15:52). The life we now live is not all there is. It is a fragment of an existence that shall stretch out into eternity. For those who trust Jesus, the tyranny of sin, death, and hell has been broken. In Christ, we understand that our departed loved ones have not passed away—they have passed on. We cherish the promise of reunion. The Resurrection touches each of us personally because it is the pledge, the promise, and the preview of our own resurrection. Christ is, as He said He was, the Resurrection and the Life (John 11:25).

*"He ascended into heaven, and sits at the
right hand of God the Father Almighty."*

Ascendit ad coelos, dedet ad dexteram Dei Patris omnipotentis

"There is a triumphant ring to the Apostles' Creed once you
reach the Ascension. At first you feel the lowliness of Jesus'
humanity, and a sting of shame in His dying like a thief.
The plunge into the depths of hell robs us of any further hope.
All seems lost. The glad surprise of the Resurrection seems
to stun even the disciples. They hardly believe their eyes.
The forty days that follow are full of assurances. The disciples
are convinced, and joy builds to a stirring climax. The
Ascension! Jesus returns to His Father, His job well-done."

Christa — Scandia, Minnesota

He Ascended

The Creed now turns from Resurrection to Ascension. Jesus made several inspiring and instructive appearances in the days after His Resurrection. However, Jesus Himself said that it was to our advantage for Him to go away.

This section of the Creed affirms the triumphant result of Christ's sinless suffering and His defeat of death and hell. Christ had overcome all that was opposed to Him. He conquered sin, both for Himself and for those who are His. By ascending to His Father, Christ opened a way for believers into the very courts of heaven.

He Sits

Unlike all that the Creed has said to this point about what Christ has undergone or accomplished, the word "sits" is in the present tense. Until now,

"*I wonder if there was a big family reunion when Jesus got back to heaven.*" **Aaron, age 8**

the Creed focused on what Jesus did in the past. Here, we see His present place and function. This is just where Jesus will remain until His return. Right now, Christ is in heaven, seated at His Father's side, ruling the universe in righteousness.

Christ is described as being seated. This implies two things. First, the task He was given on earth is completed, and He is at rest. The Son here rests in much the same way that He rested after the sixth day of creation. He finished the work of creation and turned to the task of sustaining it. Jesus, having completed His redemption of mankind, turns to His second task. Intercession. Jesus is pleading with the Father on

> "The very same hands that wield all power over the universe were once pierced by nails for the forgiveness of sin." **Emma, age 35**

our behalf (Heb. 7:24-25).

The Right Hand

"The right hand of God the Father Almighty," tells of Christ's place of honor and authority. Christ is the Lord of all, more powerful than any other worldly power. Jesus ascended to His rightful place, at the pinnacle of glory, honor, and dominion. The One who occupies it is Supreme Lord of all things. The heavens and the earth, along with all that is in them, are subject to Jesus. When the Father set the Son at His right hand, it was the coronation of the King of kings.

God's right hand is also a phrase used in Scripture to describe the destiny prepared for believers. Faith leads you to where the object of your faith has gone. In the case of Christians, this path leads to the very throne room of heaven. This is the reward of faith for all who have it. The right hand of God the Father Almighty is heaven's place of richest joy and highest honor.

Still With Us

Just because Christ reigns in heaven at the Father's right hand, do not think that He has been removed from human history. Jesus promised to be with us until the end of time. Among other things, this assurance means that the Jesus of history, our continual focus throughout the Creed thus far, is still our focus. Although He has entered the courts of heaven, and remains in His Father's presence, Jesus still remains involved in our lives. The kingship of Christ is not so very distant. It works actively among us at every moment, growing as His return draws ever closer. His promise of His presence means that He is still active. That is why Luke begins the Book of Acts by telling us that his Gospel was just an account of what Jesus began to do and to teach (Acts 1:1). Acts is Luke's account of what Jesus continued to do among us, even though He was already ascended into heaven. While He walked on this earth, He was only near a few. But now that He has ascended, He is near to us all!

Pleading and Preparing

Jesus has become the architect of our heavenly homes. He has gone ahead of His people to prepare a place for us. Jesus Christ, the Savior of the World, Conqueror of Death, King of Creation is also our heavenly advocate. Like a lawyer, He pleads our case before the Father. Jesus Christ is just the sort of attorney that we sinful people

"*As a judge, I have a unique perspective on Jesus' current activities. I see lawyers all day, everyday. Whenever I read the Apostles' Creed, I appreciate all over again that my eternal fate is in the hands of unmatchable legal representation. Christ's case for my sake is unbeatable.*"

Ray, age 52

need. He never loses a case! Of all those the Father has given to Him, He has never lost one. John's words are memorable: "If anybody sins, we have One who speaks to the Father in our defense—Jesus Christ the Righteous One" (1 John 2:1). His advocacy results in our forgiveness, and we are declared innocent in God's sight.

"From there He shall come to judge the living and the dead."

Inde venturus est iudicare vivos et mortuos.

"I wanted my girls to learn the Apostles' Creed. Audio Memory Publishing has a 'Bible Songs' tape that was helpful. The girls' favorite, though, was a song track for Steve Green's song 'We Believe.' They listened to it over and over until they could sing right along to the music themselves!"

Roxanne — Orange Grove, California

He Shall Come!

Up until now, the Creed has dealt with what Christ has done and what He is now doing on our behalf. Now, we turn to the tasks that still lie ahead. There is the future to consider. The world has not seen the last of Jesus Christ. He shall return from heaven to judge the world.

Promises of His return were always on the lips of our Lord. The disciples lived in expectation of His Coming. Paul regarded His return as an essential element of the gospel. Even the angels themselves told the apostles to expect Christ's return (Acts 1:11).

When?

There is no doubt about the Second Coming of Christ. More than 300 passages refer to it in the New Testament alone. The earliest days of the

> "*The reading of the Apostles' Creed during our evening services at church has always sent a sense of urgency running through me. In the midst of our statement of faith, comes that phrase 'He shall come,' and my heart quickens with anticipation. What if it is today?*" **Gloria, age 47**

Church were characterized by expectation and watchfulness. The worries and suffering of life were kept in perspective by the constant state of readiness in their souls.

Precisely when Christ's return shall occur no one knows. The day, the hour, the year, and even the century remain a mystery. Jesus discouraged speculation on this point. He even admitted that

He did not know the time of His return. Only God the Father is aware of the timing.

Christ's return is our hope for deliverance and a spur towards purity. Any claims of belief in the return of Christ that do not alter a Christian's behavior for the better can only be hypocritical. Too many ignore the approach of our Lord, and will be caught off guard, wrapped up in their own pointless pursuits.

Why?

There are a few purposes in Jesus' Second Coming. The New Testament affirms that Christ will gather together the people of God in order to take them as His bride. Once His preparations have been made, He will come to collect us. At His Coming, Jesus will restore all things to order, and subject them to His righteous government. Everything will be set to rights. And, He will judge the living and the dead. Of these, the Creed fixes

> "The coming judgment is a constant reminder to me that this life is really a very serious business. What I do now may have consequences that stretch out into eternity." **Max, age 27**

upon this final purpose—judgment.

Judgment

Throughout history, people of all sorts have raised up a cry for justice. Without some kind of judgment, the sinner and the saint would have identical ends. There would be no need then for pity, self-restraint, virtue, sacrifice, or even faith. Evil would run rampant. With that perspective, we thank God for judgment. We are assured that in the end, justice will be served. It is a strong deterrent to sin, and even an incentive for goodness. Christ's return to judge the living and the dead is a powerful motive for patience and courage during times of trials. It gives a steadfastness of purpose in the hour of temptation.

9

"I believe in the Holy Spirit"

Credo in Spiritum Sanctum

"I went to my pastor, confused about
all the do's and don't's that church
folks were fussing over. How could
I know what was most important?
What was absolutely necessary to
being a Christian? He showed me
a copy of the Apostles' Creed.
Now I know what the true
foundation of my faith is."

Troy — Pueblo, Colorado

The Holy Spirit

If Emmanuel was God with us, then the Holy Spirit is God in us. In the Person of the Holy Spirit, God dwells in our very hearts. He is so close to us that we often fail to distinguish His thoughts from our own. He's a behind the scenes helper, blending His work with ours. One theologian has called this His divine tact. His is an intimacy with us at the very core of our beings.

Unfortunately, the Holy Spirit is so near to us that we sometimes overlook Him. His still, small voice is easily drowned out by busyness and selfish ambition. To avoid such oversight, we must learn to recognize the Spirit's promptings. The Holy Spirit's working is easy to spot, for it will always bring glory and honor to Christ.

"I learned the Apostles' Creed in my cutechism class at church. One of the girls in my class was deaf, so we all got to learn the Creed in sign language too!" **Tracie, age 18**

Sent from the Son

Just as the Son was sent in the Father's name, so the Spirit was sent in the name of the Son. He witnesses to the glory of the Son, whose majesty He is commissioned to reveal. The Spirit testifies about what the Son has done. It comes from Him and leads to Him (John 14:25; 15:26; 16:13-15). The Spirit's task is to point us back to Christ. When you see Christ trusted, loved, and imitated, you see the Holy Spirit at work.

One of the clearest ways that the Spirit brings

glory to the Son is in our transformation. Christians are being made over again in the image of the Son. Though the process may be slow, it is truly miraculous! Nothing could bring the Son more glory than a people filled with love, joy, peace, patience, kindness, goodness, faithfulness, gentleness, and self-control (Gal. 5:22-23).

The Holy Spirit Is God

Even though the Holy Spirit has been dwelling in Christians quite intimately for centuries, He still remains something of a mystery. His subtle workings are partnered with human effort, and are apt to go unnoticed. Some Christians give Him very little thought. One thing is sure—He is God. The Holy Spirit is worshiped and glorified right along with the Father and Son.

Some of the confusion about this Person of God might arise from the varied images that Scripture uses to describe Him. Some of those images are attractive and winsome, while others are overwhelming and unapproachable: the Holy Spirit is as beautiful and gentle as a dove, as revealing and warm as a light, as awesome and overpowering as a storm, as energizing and stirring as a wind, as intense and all-consuming as a fire, and as soft and quiet as a breath or a kiss. These images are graphic and compelling. They are also hard to hold together all at once.

It helps to remember that the Spirit is indeed a living Person, multi-faceted and complex. He cannot be reduced into outline form. He has His own personality and His own ministries—He teaches, reproves, guides, speaks, testifies, comforts, and even grieves. He inspires us with new life and new desires. He renews us to repentance (Heb. 6:6). He is the great Sanctifier—He helps us glorify God.

The Holy Spirit is present most specifically in the church. In a way, He is the soul of the church.

> "I went to a Christian grade school, and every Wednesday morning we had a chapel service. As a part of the opening exercises, we would say the Pledge of Allegiance, recite The Apostles' Creed, and sing a hymn. I can still say the Apostles' Creed today." **Maria, age 35**

He is active in the hearts and minds of believers. Through the preaching of the Word, the administration of the sacraments, through the beauty of worship, in the recitation of the Word, the Holy Spirit points us to Christ.

The Trinity

The Creed affirms the existence of the Trinity.

Having previously stated belief in both the Father and the Son, it rounds out its declarations by professing belief in the Holy Spirit. However, it still maintains faith in one God. He is God in three Persons. Each is equally and fully divine, and none exist apart from the other. We must remember that the Spirit is completely God, not some lesser rank of divinity. The Father is God over us; the Son is God beside us; and the Spirit is God in us.

The Spirit's Work

The Holy Spirit aids us in several specific ways. He teaches our hearts to love the right things. Love is nothing new to our hearts, but often we fix our affections on the wrong things or in the wrong way. The Spirit restrains this waywardness as He gives insight. Through His conviction, He teaches us to love wisely.

Secondly, the Spirit teaches us when and how

> "*I have always appreciated the Apostles' Creed for its simple recitation of the truths of Christianity. I have always memorized different passages in the Bible, and I plan to learn the Creed by heart next.*" **Ron, age 44**

to pray. In fact, the Spirit Himself prays in us with words and expressions we cannot fathom. When our own words fail, His do not. Prayer is addressed to the Father by means of the way opened to us by Jesus' sacrifice. And this we do under the inspiration and guidance of the Holy Spirit, who teaches us how to pray. His is a ministry of intercession.

Third, the Holy Spirit is given the task of convicting the world of its sin and of the coming judgment (John 16:8). He brings our sins to mind so that we can confront them and conquer them by grace and repentance. He is urging us on to spiritual maturity. In the place of selfish urges, He inspires a hunger for God in our hearts. We crave intimacy with God.

Lastly, the Spirit Himself bears witness that we belong to God. He is the seal, pledge, or down payment of our salvation. We are His and He is ours.

10

"*The holy catholic church;
the communion of saints*"

sanctam ecclesiam catholicam; sanctorum communionem

∽ ∩ ∽

"I had never heard of the Apostles' Creed
until our pastor did a Sunday night sermon
series based on it. I was amazed at the history
behind its writing, and the pastor's insights
helped make it come alive for me. My wife
and I decided to memorize the Apostles'
Creed together. It has become an important
part of my devotional life."

Andrew — Seal Harbor, Maine

The Church

By His words and His deeds, Christ made it clear that He would build a church (Matt. 16:18). He gave it a band of carefully selected and specially trained leaders. He gave it a mission and a message. He gave it rituals of entrance and of remembrance, which He said were to endure until He returned. He gave it rules of discipline and the authority to enforce them. He even gave it an entire Testament full of written instructions for its future guidance. He bought it with His own blood. He intercedes for it. He sustains it. He will return to gather it to Himself. He declared that He would build His church and promised that even the gates of hell, which could not hold Him, would not hold it.

> "My church family, especially the members of my Sunday school class, are closer to me than most of my real family! They know me better. They understand my heart." **Sue Ann, age 36**

Changes over Time

In its earliest days, the church was small, simple, and passionate. It was a courageous fellowship in faith. The early believers fully intended to spread this Good News to the whole world. However, soon financial difficulties, administrative disputes, theological disagreements, political oppression, and ethnic divisions began to crop up (Acts 2:43-47; 5:12-16; 6:1-7; 15:1-29). To address these problems effectively, the church had to get organized. In the course of a single century, the church became something very different than what the Apostles had established.

The church became more liturgical and administrative. Complex theological issues had to be defined. In short, it became a highly organized institution. Individual congregations became more geographically and culturally diverse. In time, the church became the churches, with numerous denominations replacing its original simplicity.

Today, we must not identify the church with the many individual churches worldwide. It would be impossible to define the church by the rituals, buildings, geographical locations, histories, hierarchies, funds, and organizational structures of so many denominations. The church consists of believers and the One in whom they believe. Membership in one does not necessarily guarantee membership in the other. The church is made up of all believers who exercise faith in Christ.

The church will never pass away. It will survive all catastrophes. It will endure any setbacks. This isn't because of its own powers or tenacity, but because of its foundation—Jesus Christ, Who is the same yesterday, today, and forever (Heb. 13:8). To speak of its endurance through all time is to believe in Him through Whom and by Whom it endures. He is her cornerstone.

The Visible and the Invisible

Our churches today have two dimensions. The invisible dimension is made up only of true believers. Only people of faith are included. This is the true church. On the other hand, the visible churches contain believers and unbelievers alike. Though many are saved, many are still searching.

These various churches and their denominations function to help the church to fulfill its mission of making disciples (Matt. 28:16-20). These churches bring the gospel to their members and to the world. Churches are a means by which a broken and fallen world can be served. Churches are places where believers interact with one another and grow toward maturity.

Holy

As defined by the Creed, the identifying marks of the church are holiness and catholicity. The word "holy" does not imply moral purity. It means "set apart for God's service." The church is not holy because its members are pure—they are not. If holy meant "pure" then the church would be empty, for no one is truly pure. Rather, believers are set apart for God's work. They are not without faults, but they have given themselves in faith to Jesus Christ. They are holy by virtue of their Lord and their calling, not their purity. The church's glory and holiness lie in her consecration to God.

"*One day it struck me that when we all got to heaven, my daughter will be my sister. So will my mother. Even my grandmother will be a sister to me in Christ. My husband will be my brother. So will my son. Somehow, understanding this family aspect of Christianity has deepened my love for my Christian friends and family.*" **Debra, age 30**

Catholic

The word "catholic" is widely misunderstood. It has nothing to do with the Roman Catholic faith. The original meaning of this word was "universal." The church is universal with respect to time, place, doctrine, and mission. It has a universal character. It is meant for all nations and all time.

"My uncle was a missionary for years in West Africa. Though my brother and I saved up money to put in the missions offering and sent our hand-me-downs in boxes overseas, I don't think I realized for years that the people over there were part of my church family. Because they were needy, I guess I thought they were less Christian than I was. Now I know better, and I am both amazed and proud that I have Christian brothers and sisters all over the world. I can't wait to meet them someday in heaven." **Dwayne, age 27**

In saying that the church is catholic, we affirm

that its message is valid and relevant in every age and in every situation. God has given us one church and one gospel for all time. So, the same church seeks to apply the same gospel to what ever situation in which it happens to find itself.

To speak of the church's catholicity is to speak of its universality—one Lord, one faith. Too slowly, Christians from many different backgrounds and denominations have come to realize that what they have in common is far more precious and important than what divides them.

Communion of the Saints

"Communion" here does not refer to the Lord's Supper. It simply means fellowship. The communion of the Saints is the fellowship of the faithful, the comradeship of believers. This fellowship is so durable that it cannot be severed by time, distance, or even death.

The Christian is not an isolated individual. He

is not designed to stand alone. The concept of a Christian hermit is a contradiction in terms. No believer is alone because he is united forever with Christ and to all other Christians. Communion is to be drawn out of one's isolation and to be planted into the unity and love of the body of Christ. To be a part of the communion of saints is to become one of God's people, chosen by God to serve Him, to know Him, and to enjoy Him forever.

It is a wide community, stretching into both the past and the future. We have fellow believers who lived before us and who are yet to come. We have friends in high places and friends who have little in this world. They are our family in the faith, both our spiritual ancestry and our posterity.

This phrase in the Creed reminds us of those who gave their lives and hearts to Christ and His gospel. It brings to our minds the highest deeds, the worthiest actions, the profoundest sufferings and the grandest loves of all who came before us.

"*We moved away from our church family after ten years of fellowship. Goodbyes were hard, and tears were shed. Even though we are hundreds of miles away from them now, the fellowship remains. We connect through letters and through prayers. I know someday we will all be reunited for eternity.*" **Gayle, age 41**

When we think of these, we are heartened and strengthened. We are indebted to those who counted no cost too high in their quest to glorify God. We pray that our own example might be as instructive and inspiring for those who follow us. We are part of something bigger than ourselves. We are not alone.

"The forgiveness of sins"

remissionem peccatorum

"I always admired my Grandmother's
memory. She could quote whole poems,
and for every poem she would recite, she
would tell a passage of Scripture. She
could tell the story of Christmas from
Luke right off the top of her head. She
knew dozens of Psalms. And, she would
recite the Apostles' Creed for me.
I think it was one of her favorites."

Lena — Boise, Idaho

What Is Sin?

Sin is a fact of life. Regardless of country, century, or culture, sin is one of the chief and enduring characteristics of earthly existence. Every history text and every news report bears eloquent and undeniable testimony to human depravity. Even in our best moments, noble deeds are tainted by ulterior motives. This bothers us, but probably not as much as it should. We are conscious of the difference between right and wrong, and we are aware when the line between them has been crossed.

In Scripture, the word "sin" has many meanings—missing the target, failing to be what we ought to be, stepping across a line, trespassing, stumbling, falling, breaking the law, disobeying, ignoring Commandments, moral debt. Sin is multi-faceted. However, its many dimensions can be reduced to this: Sin is whatever is contrary to

> *"Sin is always destructive to the sinner. Even in a good man, it will cloud his intellect, poison his imagination, weaken his will, and deaden his conscience."* **Mortimer,** The Creeds

the righteous will of God.

None of us escapes from evil. None of us is truly righteous. We are a fallen race. Sin is the condition of every human soul everywhere. In the words of Scripture, all of us have sinned and fallen short of God's glory (Rom. 3:23).

Sin and Sinning

Theologians often distinguish between sin and sins. The first is the condition of spiritual death, the second is the wicked action or conduct

"*Medieval sculptors often portrayed sin from the front as a handsome young man, beckoning the unsuspecting to indulge themselves in what promises to be innocent fun. From behind, those sculptors portrayed sin either as a writhing nest of vipers or as a withered and ugly skeleton, the personification of death and putrefaction. In other words, sin never practices truth in advertising.*"

Timothy, age 40

that arises from that condition.

Sin is an attempt to satisfy a legitimate need in an illegitimate manner. We are slow to learn that sin is ultimately unsatisfying. It promises one thing and delivers another. It promises happiness, it delivers guilt, shame, doubt, alienation, and spiritual death

Just forgiving our many sins will not cure all that ails us. The condition that spawns such actions is still in place. New sins will quickly replace the sins that are washed away. Purification must take place. The Christian convert becomes a new person at the very heart, having new hopes, new desires, new loves, new aspirations, and new modes of conduct. Old things are done away with and new things grow up in their place (2 Cor. 5:17).

God's Perspective on Sin

God does not treat sin the way we do. God does not excuse sin, and He does not condone it. He judges it. He eradicates sin, root and branch, at a high cost to Himself. However, the sentence He passes upon sin is a sentence He Himself has borne. He does not compromise. To forgive sin is not to ignore it or to downplay it. It is to take it upon oneself in much the same way that a creditor must pay for every outstanding debt owed him, but which he elects to cancel. The cost of the bad loan is borne, though not by the borrower.

The Wages of Sin

Sin is an employer for whom we all work and by whom we all get paid. The payment we receive for our sin is death (Rom. 6:23). The more you sin, the more likely you are not to feel its sting. If you cannot feel sin's approach, you cannot arm yourself against it. If you no longer feel pangs of conscience once you commit sin, you are stripped of the remorse that makes you determined not to repeat your mistakes. Without that determination, you sin still more. In this way, sin breeds sin.

God is completely pure, and so He must deal with sin. There are only two choices. He either punishes sin or forgives it. As a result, each of us stands in desperate need of mercy and grace. In the New Testament, to forgive sins means to cover them, to send them away, to blot them out. We stand in need of forgiveness.

Forgiveness

From the Creed we learn another thing about God the Father Almighty, maker of heaven and earth—He forgives. Our Maker is our Redeemer. If God wasn't merciful, we would be utterly undone.

The cure for sin is not moral reform, but forgiveness. Forgiveness means that Christ has taken our place. He has stood in our stead and received the punishment we deserved. His death in our place permits us to go free. Our punishment has been paid.

Our forgiveness is based upon the saving work of God in Christ. It rests upon the death of Jesus on our behalf. It costs us nothing. It cost

God everything. It is free, but it is not cheap. Forgiveness was provided by Jesus. He saved us by His righteous life and atoning death. He paid our penalty. God puts Himself in the place of the sinner. He died so that we might live.

Repentance

Forgiveness also has a human dimension to it. Our forgiveness also hinges upon our repentance, our confession and our readiness to forgive. Repentance is not the same as regret or as the desire to escape punishment. That would only be fear. We are to repent of our sins, not merely fear their consequences.

In the New Testament, "repentance" means literally to have an afterthought, to think again, or to reassess one's actions. Put differently, repentance is a U-turn, an about-face, a radical change of heart regarding one's sinful actions. There is no forgiveness without a truly repentant heart. To

"*Some people treat me like a goody-two shoes because I'm a Christian. They seem to think I'm 'Miss Perfect' and accuse me of having a holier-than-thou attitude. The teasing is hard to react to. What can I say? I'm not perfect. I'm just forgiven!*" **Nancy, age 27**

wish to have God's forgiveness without this about-face is impudence.

Confession

To confess means, literally, to speak along with or to agree with someone. To confess one's sins is to say about them what God says about them. It is to agree with God that those sins are indeed evil. It is admitting that you have done something wrong and have taken responsibility for it. You must own your sin. Forgiveness depends upon sinners seeing sin as sin. If we confess our sins, the Bible says, God is faithful and just and will forgive us our sins and cleanse us from all unrighteousness (1 John 1:9).

Forgive One Another

Finally, we must be forgiving if we are to be forgiven. As recipients of God's mercy, God expects us to be merciful. Someone who would withhold forgiveness from his brother cannot expect to receive it from God (Matt. 5:7, 6:14-15). The possibility of forgiveness goes hand-in-hand with being forgiving.

If you repent, confess, and forgive, God will forgive you. He will pardon your offenses and never call them to mind again (Jer. 31:34).

"The resurrection of the body, and life everlasting"

carnis resurrectionem; vitam aeternam

"As a youngster, learning my memory verses and catechisms was a bit boring and tedious. Now, when I say the Apostles' Creed, I feel a feeling of triumph. It's not from a sense of accomplishment though. It's anticipation, for the last words of the Creed are a promise: life everlasting."

Samuel — Plains, Georgia

Resurrection

The last words of the Creed contain two affirmations. In its parting declaration, we are given words of unparalleled hope and confidence. The victory to which the Creed here refers is total.

This is the second time that resurrection is brought up. The first was the Resurrection of Jesus. The second will be ours. He is the firstfruits of those who are raised from the dead (1 Cor. 15:23). The Spirit Who raised Him shall raise us (Rom. 8:11). We will follow where Christ has led. Though He was dead, yet He lives. So shall we.

A Glorified Body

Much as a seed is planted in the ground and by its decay gives rise to a stalk of corn or a mighty oak, the physical body that we lay in the grave decays and gives rise to a spiritual body. We

"The Apostles' Creed is important to me because my God is important to me. It helps me to understand Him better." **Jennifer, age 13**

will leave death and weakness behind, and take on a body suited for eternity. Paul reminded us that what is sown is perishable, but what is raised is imperishable. What is sown in dishonor is raised in glory. What is sown in weakness is raised in power. It is sown a physical body; it is raised a spiritual body (1 Cor. 15:42-44).

Our bodies allow us to exist at a particular place and to come into contact with the world around us. Our bodies are our means of self-expression. Bodies make possible our interaction with others. To say that we are to have bodies in the resurrected life means that we will be then

> "I miss my Grandpa. He died when I was really little. Grandma tells me stories about him, and that helps me remember him better. When I get to heaven, he will be there. I'll tell him all about me, so that he can remember me better."
>
> **Logan, age 5**

what we are now—real persons capable of real life. We shall be genuine, solid authentic human beings. Our complete identity shall be preserved. We shall be fully human—more human than we are now. We lose nothing at death but our sin and its attendant hindrances.

In other words, we anticipate the resurrection of the whole person, not simply a disembodied soul. Nor will it be a resurrection like that of

Lazarus, who was raised only to die again. Having died once, we shall put death forever behind us.

Life Everlasting

Christ's defeat of death teaches us that our earthly life is just a preface to our eternal life. This life is not all there is. The grave that awaits us is a doorway, a beginning, and not an end. The life to come will be the death of death.

What the Scripture normally calls eternal life, the Creed calls "life everlasting."

This does not refer to longevity of life, but to a special quality of life. This is life that comes from knowing God and living in communion with Him. According to Scripture, eternal life entails knowing and abiding in God (1 John 5:20). In Peter's words, eternal life is our participation in God's own divine nature (2 Pet. 1:4).

Eternal life is not the same as mere immortality or endless existence, though those are included within it. Eternal life must be understood as divine life, as extraordinary life, the life of God shared by His creation. Eternal life is our life with Him Who is Life (John 11:25).

Anticipating Eternity

Considering these points fills us with a joyful anticipation, knowing that someday we will be precisely what our all-wise Creator intended us to be. In the face of this infinite joy, we learn not to toy with the meager and shallow pleasures of sin, which can only hurt us.

Eternal life is the final chapter of the world's great saga—a saga written by the Hand of God. That chapter brings the end of sorrow, pain, evil, and doubt. Eternal life is God's final word to us—not death, not annihilation, but life. That is the Creed's final word to us as well. Where the Creed leaves off, the life to come is just beginning. Epilogue is but prologue after all.